This edition published 1995 by Geddes & Grosset Ltd,
David Dale House, New Lanark, Scotland

Illustrated by Lyndsay Duff in the style of Charles Robinson

ISBN 1 85534 561 7

Printed in Slovenia

**Mother Goose Rhymes**

London
Bridge

## *London Bridge*

London Bridge is broken down,
Dance o'er my Lady Lee;
London Bridge is broken down,
With a gay lady.

How shall we build it up again?
Dance o'er my Lady Lee;
How shall we build it up again?
With a gay lady.

Silver and gold will be stole away,
Dance o'er my Lady Lee;
Silver and gold will be stole away,
With a gay lady.

Build it up again with iron and steel,
Dance o'er my Lady Lee;
Build it up with iron and steel,
With a gay lady.

Iron and steel will bend and bow,
Dance o'er my Lady Lee;
Iron and steel will bend and bow,
With a gay lady.

Build it up with wood and clay,
Dance o'er my Lady Lee;
Build it up with wood and clay,
With a gay lady.

Wood and clay will wash away,
Dance o'er my Lady Lee;
Wood and clay will wash away,
With a gay lady.

Build it up with stone so strong,
Dance o'er my Lady Lee;
Huzza! 't will last for ages long,
With a gay lady.

# The FOX and the GOOSE

THE fox and his wife they had a great strife,
They never ate mustard in all their whole life;
They ate their meat without fork or knife,
And loved to be picking a bone, e-ho!

## *The Fox and the Goose*

The fox jumped up on a moonlight night;
The stars they were shining, and all things bright;
"Oh, ho!" said the fox, "it 's a very fine night
For me to go through the town, e-ho!"

The fox when he came to yonder stile,
He lifted his lugs and he listened a while;
"Oh, ho!" said the fox, "it 's but a short mile
From this into yonder wee town, e-ho!"

## *The Fox and the Goose*

The fox when he came to the farmer's gate,
Whom should he see but the farmer's drake;
"I love you well for your master's sake,
    And long to be picking your bones, e-ho!"

The gray goose she ran round the hay-stack;
"Oh, ho!" said the fox, "you are very fat,
You 'll grease my beard and ride on my back
    From this into yonder wee town, e-ho!"

The farmer's wife she jumped out of bed,
And out of the window she popped her head;
"Oh, husband! oh, husband! the geese are all dead,
    For the fox has been through the town, e-ho!"

Then the old man got up in his red cap,
And swore he would catch the fox in a trap;
But the fox was too cunning, and gave him the slip,
    And ran through the town, the town, e-ho!

When he got to the top of the hill,
He blew his trumpet both loud and shrill,
For joy that he was in safety still,
And had got away through the town, e-ho!

When the fox came back to his den,
He had young ones both nine and ten;
"You 're welcome home, daddy; you may go again,
If you bring us such fine meat from the town,
e-ho!"

# WHERE ARE YOU GOING?

"WHERE are you going to, my pretty maid?"

"I'm going a-milking, sir," she said.

## *Where are you going?*

"May I go with you, my pretty maid?"
"You 're kindly welcome, sir," she said.

"What is your father, my pretty maid?"
"My father 's a farmer, sir," she said.

"What is your fortune, my pretty maid?"
"My face is my fortune, sir," she said.

"Then I can't marry you, my pretty maid!"
"Nobody asked you, sir," she said.

# KING PIPPIN'S HALL

KING PIPPIN built a fine new hall,
Pastry and pie-crust were the wall;
Windows made of black pudding
and white,
Slates were pancakes, you ne'er
saw the like.

# IF

If all the world were apple-
pie,
And all the water ink,
What should we do for bread
and cheese?
What should we do for
drink?

# COFFEE AND TEA

MOLLY, my sister, and I
fell out,
And what do you think
it was about?
She loved coffee and I
loved tea,
And that was the reason we couldn't agree.

## THE CROOKED SONG

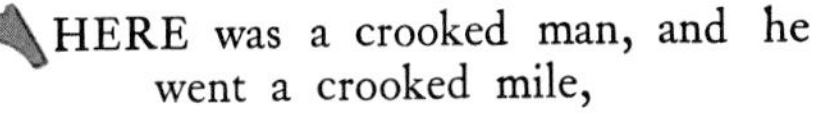

THERE was a crooked man, and he
went a crooked mile,
He found a crooked sixpence beside
a crooked stile;
He bought a crooked cat, which
caught a crooked mouse,
And they all lived together in a
little crooked house.

## A, B, C

A, B, C, tumble down D,
The cat 's in the cupboard
And can't see me.

# Comical Folk

IN a cottage in Fife
Lived a man and his wife,
Who, believe me, were comical folk;
For, to people's surprise,
They both saw with their eyes,
And their tongues moved whenever they spoke.

When they were asleep,
I 'm told—that to keep
Their eyes open they could not contrive;
They both walked on their feet,
And 't was thought what they eat
Helped, with drinking, to keep them alive.

# A WONDERFUL THING

AS I went to Bonner,
I met a pig
Without a wig,
Upon my word and honour.

# MY BOY TAMMIE

"WHERE have you been
all day,
My boy Tammie?"
"I 've been all the day
Courting of a lady gay;
But oh, she 's too young
To be taken from her mammy!"

"What work can she do,
My boy Tammie?
Can she bake and can she brew,
My boy Tammie?"

"She can brew and she can bake,
And she can make our wedding cake;
But oh, she 's too young
To be taken from her mammy!"

"What age may she be?
What age may she be,
My boy Tammie?"

"Twice two, twice seven,
Twice ten, twice eleven;
But oh, she 's too young
To be taken from her mammy!"

# THE WIND ·

When the wind is in the East,
'T is neither good for man nor beast;
When the wind is in the North,
The skilful fisher goes not forth;
When the wind is in the South,
It blows the bait in the fish's mouth;
When the wind is in the West,
Then 't is at the very best.

# ROBIN AND RICHARD

Robin and Richard were two little men,
They did not awake till the clock struck ten;

Then up starts Robin, and looks at the sky;
Oh! brother Richard, the sun 's very high!

They both were ashamed, on such a fine day,
When they were wanted to make the new hay.

Do you go before, with bottle and bag,
I will come after on little Jack nag.

# THE LITTLE MAN WITH A GUN

There was a little man, and he had a little gun,
And his bullets were made of lead, lead, lead;
He went to the brook, and saw a little duck,
And shot it right through the head, head, head.

He carried it home to his old wife Joan,
And bade her a fire to make, make, make,
To roast the little duck he had shot in the brook,
And he'd go and fetch the drake, drake, drake.

The drake was a-swimming, with his curly tail;
The little man made it his mark, mark, mark.
He let off his gun, but he fired too soon,
And the drake flew away with a quack, quack, quack.

# IF WISHES WERE HORSES

If wishes were horses, beggars would ride;
If turnips were watches, I would wear
one by my side.

# CLAP HANDIES

Clap, clap handies,
Mammie's wee, wee ain;
Clap, clap handies,
Daddie 's comin' hame;
Hame till his bonny
wee bit laddie;
Clap, clap handies,
My wee, wee ain.

## ANDREW

AS I was going o'er Westminster Bridge,
I met with a Westminster scholar;
He pulled off his cap, *an' drew* off his glove,
And wished me a very good morrow.
What is his name?

## MARY'S CANARY

Mary had a pretty bird,
Feathers bright and yellow;
Slender legs—upon my word,
He was a pretty fellow.
The sweetest note he always sung,
Which much delighted Mary;
She often, where the cage was hung,
Sat hearing her canary.

# THE CUCKOO

In April,
Come he will.

In May,
He sings all day.

In June,
He changes his tune.

In July,
He prepares to fly.

In August,
Go he must.

# A SWARM OF BEES

A swarm of bees in May
Is worth a load of hay;
A swarm of bees in June
Is worth a silver spoon;
A swarm of bees in July
Is not worth a fly.

# TOM THE PIPER'S SON

Tom, Tom, the piper's son,
He learned to play when he was young,
But all the tune that he could play
Was "Over the hills and far away".
Over the hills, and a great way off,
And the wind will blow my top-knot off.

Now Tom with his pipe made such a noise
That he pleased both the girls and boys,
And they stopped to hear him play
"Over the hills and far away".

Tom with his pipe did play with such skill
That those who heard him could never stand still;
Whenever they heard they began for to dance,
Even pigs on their hind-legs would after him prance.

## *Tom the Piper's Son*

As Dolly was milking the cow one day,
Tom took out his pipe and began for to play;
So Doll and the cow danced "the Cheshire round",
Till the pail was broke, and the milk ran on the ground.

He met old Dame Trot with a basket of eggs,
He used his pipe, and she used her legs;
She danced about till the eggs were all broke,
She began for to fret, but he laughed at the joke.

He saw a cross fellow was beating an ass,
Heavy laden with pots, pans, dishes, and glass;
He took out his pipe and played them a tune,
And the jack-ass's load was lightened full soon.

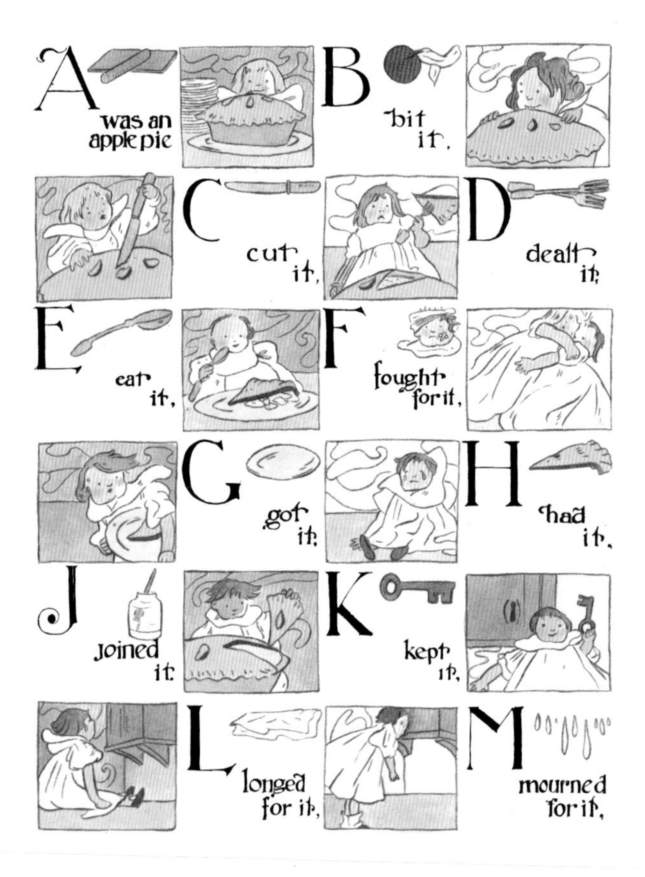
A
was an
apple pie
B
bit
it,
C
cut
it,
D
dealt
it;
E
eat
it,
F
fought
for it,
G
got
it;
H
had
it,
J
joined
it;
K
kept
it,
L
longed
for it,
M
mourned
for it,